Chemicals
in Action

Acids &
Bases

Chris Oxlade

Heinemann Library
Chicago, Illinois

Designed by Tinstar Design
Illustrations by Jeff Edwards
Originated by Ambassador Litho
Printed by Wing King Tong in Hong Kong

06 05 04 03 02
10 9 8 7 6 5 4 3 2 1

Library of Congress Cataloging-in-Publication Data
Oxlade, Chris.
  Acids and bases / Chris Oxlade.
      p. cm. -- (Chemicals in action)
Includes bibliographical references and index.
  ISBN 1-58810-194-0
  1. Acid-base chemistry--Juvenile literature. [1. Chemistry. 2. Acids.
3. Bases (Chemistry)] I. Title.
  QD477 .O95 2001
  546'.24--dc21

                              2001000102

Acknowledgments
The author and publishers are grateful to the following for permission to reproduce copyright material: pp. 4, 9, 12, 18, 28, 34 Science Photo Library; p. 5 TDG Nexus/Mark Perry/Simon Peachey; pp. 6, 10, 32, 36 Roger Scruton; pp. 8, 15, 17, 20, 23, 25, 27, 29, 37 Trevor Clifford; pp. 11, 24 Peter Gould; pp. 13, 22, 35 Corbis; pp. 14, 16, 33 Andrew Lambert; p. 19 Edifice; pp. 30, 39 Robert Harding; p. 31 Ace Photo Library; p. 38 Environmental Images/Toby Adamson.

Cover photograph: Science Photo Library/Charles D Winters

The publishers would like to thank Ted Dolter and Dr. Nigel Saunders for their assistance in the preparation of this book.

Every effort has been made to contact copyright holders of any material reproduced in this book. Any omissions will be rectified in subsequent printings if notice is given to the publisher.

Some words are shown in bold, **like this.** You can find out what they mean by looking in the glossary.

Contents

Chemicals in Action

What's the link between **corrosion,** cleaning the kitchen, bee stings, fire fighting, and indigestion? The answer is acids and bases. All these things use or contain acids or bases, or happen because of acids or bases. Our knowledge of how acids and bases behave is used in making chemicals, in farming, in engineering, and at home.

The study of acids and bases is part of the science of chemistry. Many people think of chemistry as something that scientists study by doing experiments in laboratories with special equipment. This part of chemistry is very important. It is how scientists find out what substances are made of and how they make new materials—but this is only a tiny part of chemistry. Most chemistry happens away from laboratories, in factories and chemical plants. It is used to manufacture an enormous range of items, such as synthetic fibers for fabrics, drugs to treat diseases, explosives for fireworks, solvents for paints, and **fertilizers** for growing crops.

Many acids and bases are natural. The water in this lake in a volcano in Costa Rica is acidic.

About the activities

There are several activities in the book for you to try. They will help you to understand some of the chemistry in the book. Some of the activities are demonstrations. Doing them will demonstrate a scientific concept. The other activities are experiments. An experiment is designed to help solve a scientific problem. Scientists use a logical approach to experiments so that they can conclude things from the results of the experiments. A scientist first develops a hypothesis, which might be the answer to the problem, then designs an experiment to test the hypothesis. He or she then observes the results of the experiment and concludes whether or not the results show the hypothesis to be correct. We know what we do about chemistry because scientists have carried out millions of experiments over hundreds of years. Experiments have helped us to understand why different substances are solids, liquids, and gases and why they have the **properties** they do.

Doing the activities

All the activities in this book have been designed for you to do at home with everyday substances and equipment. They can also be done in a school laboratory. Always follow the safety advice given with each activity, and ask an adult to help you when the instructions tell you to.

Acids or bases can be dangerous. Flasks, canisters, and tankers that contain them must display a hazard warning.

About Acids and Bases

Acids and bases are chemicals, and you probably have seen bottles of both in your school laboratory. An alkali is simply a base that **dissolves** in water. You might also recognize some names of acids, bases, and alkalis, such as sulfuric acid and sodium hydroxide.

Acids, bases, and alkalis are not chemicals that are found only in bottles in laboratories. There are hundreds of natural acids, bases, and alkalis in plants and animals. For example, lemon juice contains an acid called citric acid, and you have hydrochloric acid in your stomach that is so strong it could eat away **metal!** Even wasp stings contain alkalis. Hundreds of everyday substances such as shampoo, vinegar, spray-on cleaners, and even rainwater are acids, bases, or alkalis. Acids, bases, and alkalis are also found in medicines such as antacids, and you can often see their names in the list of ingredients on packaging.

In factories, acids, bases, and alkalis are used to clean materials such as metal and are the **raw materials** that make hundreds of other chemicals, such as **fertilizers** and **detergents.**

Strong oven cleaners contain strong acids or alkalis. It is important to wear protective gloves when using them.

Acid, base, and alkali reactions

Acids, bases, and alkalis can eat away other substances or make them fizz because there is a **chemical reaction** between them. For example, when acids come into contact with some metals, the metal is eaten away and bubbles of hydrogen are formed. Cleaning liquids that contain alkalis work because the alkali reacts with grease, turning it into other substances.

Safety with acids, bases, and alkalis

Although natural acids, bases, and alkalis are usually harmless to touch and eat, some acids, bases, and alkalis found in the laboratory and in household cleaners are dangerous. They are described as **corrosive** or **caustic,** meaning that they will eat away some materials—including your skin. Look out for hazard warning symbols on chemicals in the laboratory and at home, and never touch or taste any acids, bases, or alkalis (or any other chemicals) unless you have been told by a scientist or other adult that it is safe to do so. Always wear safety glasses when using acids, bases, or alkalis.

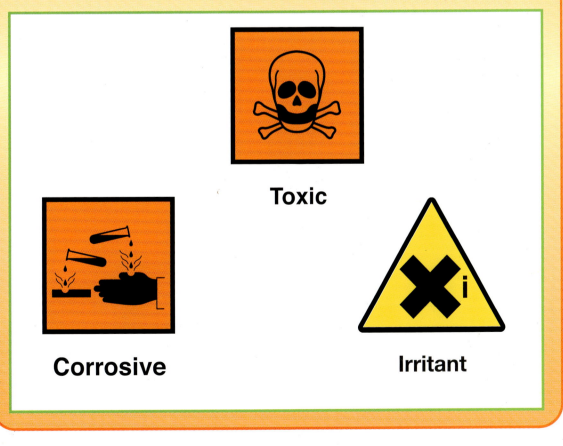

Toxic

Corrosive

Irritant

Acids

The word acid comes from the Latin word *acidus,* meaning sour. Sour is the sharp taste in fruits such as lemons and oranges. One of the **properties** of an acid is that is it tastes sour—this is how acids got their name. Lemons and oranges taste sour because they contain a weak acid, called citric acid, that is safe to taste. You should never taste an acid (or any other chemical) unless you are told that it is safe to do so by a scientist or other responsible adult.

The other properties of acids are:
- acids are usually found **dissolved** in water
- acids can eat away other substances, such as **metals,** and they are described as **corrosive**
- acids are **neutralized** by alkalis and bases, meaning that they are turned into a substance that is no longer an acid
- acids have a **pH** below 7, and they also turn blue **litmus** paper red.

Carbonated drinks are acidic. They can even be used to clean dirty coins!

Laboratory acids

The most common acids that scientists use in the laboratory are sulfuric acid, hydrochloric acid, and nitric acid. These are also the most common acids used in industry. The **chemical formulas** for these acids are:

sulfuric acid	H_2SO_4
hydrochloric acid	HCl
nitric acid	HNO_3

You can see from these formulas that all acids contain hydrogen. It is the hydrogen that gives them their special properties. The formulas do not tell you one very important thing, and that is that the chemicals must be dissolved in water before they have the properties of acids. For example, hydrochloric acid is made up of hydrogen chloride (HCl) dissolved in water. Pure hydrogen chloride is a gas, not an acid, but it is called an **acidic gas** because it dissolves in water to make an acid.

Strong and weak acids

Acids are called either strong or weak, depending on how vigorously they react with other substances. Sulfuric acid, which is found in car batteries, is a strong acid. The acetic acid found in vinegar is a weak acid, like most other acids found in foods.

An acid can also be labeled **concentrated** or **dilute,** depending on how much solvent has been added. The more water added, the more dilute the acid becomes. Concentrated strong acids are very dangerous and should be handled with the greatest care. But even concentrated weak acids can be dangerous. The acid in vinegar is diluted, so it is safe to consume. Diluted strong acids are also much less dangerous, and are often used in the home.

Concentrated sulfuric acid is nasty stuff! It dehydrates (removes the water from) sugar instantly.

Bases and Alkalis

You can think of bases and alkalis as the chemical opposites of acids. A base is any substance that will **neutralize** an acid. This means that adding a base to an acid eventually turns the acid into liquid that's not an acid. It changes the acid's **properties.**

The word alkali means simply a base that will **dissolve** in water, or, more often, is dissolved in water to make a **solution.** Some bases do not dissolve in water. They are called **insoluble bases.** This means that all alkalis are also bases, but only bases that dissolve in water are alkalis. For example, magnesium oxide and calcium oxide are both bases because they both neutralize acids. But magnesium oxide does not dissolve in water, so it cannot be an alkali, too. Calcium oxide dissolves in water, so it is an alkali.

Properties of alkalis

The most obvious property of an alkali is that it feels soapy or slimy to touch. You should never touch (or taste) an alkali unless you are told that it is safe to do so by a scientist or other adult.

Some alkalis and bases are good cleaning agents. This liquid contains the base ammonia (NH_3).

Other properties of alkalis are:

- alkalis can eat away other substances, and they are described as **corrosive**
- alkalis are neutralized by acids, meaning that an acid turns an alkali into a substance that is no longer an alkali
- alkalis have a **pH** above 7, and they also turn red **litmus** paper blue.

The word alkali comes from the Arabic *al-qili,* a word for the ashes made when certain plants are burned. These ashes were people's first source of alkalis.

Laboratory bases and alkalis

The most common bases that scientists use in the laboratory are sodium hydroxide and calcium hydroxide. They are both alkalis, too—in fact, they are also the most common alkalis used in industry. Sodium hydroxide is also known as **caustic** soda, and calcium hydroxide is also known as slaked lime.

The **chemical formulas** for these alkalis are:

sodium hydroxide	NaOH
calcium hydroxide	Ca(OH)$_2$

You can see from these formulas that alkalis contain hydrogen and oxygen combined into a hydroxyl (OH), and it is this hydroxyl that gives them their properties. The formulas do not tell you one very important thing, and that is that the chemicals must be dissolved in water before they show the properties of alkalis. For example, the alkali sodium hydroxide is made up of sodium hydroxide, a solid, dissolved in water. Solid sodium hydroxide is not an alkali, but it is called an **alkaline** solid because it dissolves in water to make an alkaline solution.

The base calcium oxide dissolves in water to make an alkaline solution that turns litmus paper blue.

Natural Acids and Bases

All plants and animals contain thousands of chemicals, including many acids, bases, and alkalis. These acids, bases, and alkalis play a part in important processes that allow plants and animals to live and grow, such as **digestion.** Some plants and animals also use acids, bases, and alkalis for self-defense. Here you can find out about some of these naturally occurring acids, bases, and alkalis.

Acids and bases in your body

Did you know that your stomach is like a bag full of acid? It contains up to a pint (half a liter) of hydrochloric acid that helps you to digest food! The acid is part of a liquid called gastric juice that helps to break down the complex chemicals found in food into simpler substances that your body can digest. Hydrochloric acid also kills any bacteria on the food and is strong enough to **dissolve metals** and burn skin. Fortunately, your stomach has a special lining that protects it from the acid, and your body also makes alkalis that **neutralize** the acid so that it doesn't eat away your intestines!

Your body also uses different acids to grow and work. Vitamin C is a chemical that helps to heal wounds and grow skin and healthy bones, but it is actually an acid called ascorbic acid. Fruit and vegetables are important sources of vitamin C.

Plants called stinging nettles inject a tiny bit of acid into your skin!

Some acids in your body are made by other **organisms,** including the bacteria that live in your mouth and feed on tiny pieces of food. They produce acid that can eat away at your teeth, causing decay. Regular brushing prevents too much bacterial growth.

Acid and base stings

Ants, bees, and nettles can all sting you by injecting tiny amounts of acid into your skin. Ants inject formic acid, also known as methanoic acid. Wasp stings, on the other hand, contain a base instead of an acid. Stings swell up because your body sends water to the area of the sting to try to **dilute** the acid or base. Acids and bases are also used to treat bites and stings. They do this by neutralizing the substance in the sting.

Naturally occurring calcium carbonate is turned into lime using fire at this lime kiln.

Making lime

Calcium **carbonate** ($CaCO_3$) is a chemical that makes up many types of rock, including chalk and limestone. It is a base and is an important **raw material** for the chemical industry. Heating calcium carbonate makes it decompose into carbon dioxide and calcium oxide, commonly known as lime. Lime was one of the first human-made chemicals and it has been used since Roman times to make cement for building.

Testing Acids and Bases

Scientists often need to find out whether a substance is an acid, a base, or neutral. A neutral substance is a substance that is neither an acid nor a base.

Scientists test substances using chemicals called **indicators.** When an indicator is put into a liquid, it changes color to show whether the liquid is an acid, a base, or neutral. Some indicators show only whether a liquid is an acid or a base, while others show how strong an acid or base is. Indicators can only be used with liquids, so you can't test any solid substances with an indicator.

Acid or base?

Litmus is an indicator that shows whether a liquid is an acid or a base. It comes in the form of paper strips, called litmus paper, or in a **solution.** Here's what happens when litmus paper is dipped in acids, bases, and neutral liquids:

	In acid	In base	In neutral
Red litmus	Stays red	Turns blue	Stays red
Blue litmus	Turns red	Stays blue	Stays blue

*Red litmus paper turns blue when it is dipped into an **alkaline** solution.*

Experiment: Natural indicators

PROBLEM: Can acids and bases be tested without litmus paper?

HYPOTHESIS: The chemical dyes in litmus paper come from a plant, so there might be similar dyes in other plants as well. Extracting dyes from plants and adding them to acids and bases will show if they are indicators.

Experiment steps

1. Pull some large leaves from the outside of a red cabbage, tear them into small strips, and put them into a bowl. Ask an adult to help you pour about a pint (half a liter) of boiling water over the leaves.

2. Let the water and cabbage mixture cool for about half an hour before pouring it through a strainer into a large jar. This liquid is your indicator.

3. Add a few drops of the indicator to a small jar of tap water and to another of white wine vinegar (a weak acid). Note the color changes for both.

RESULTS: What colors does the cabbage juice turn in the tap water and the weak acid? Are the colors the same? What do you think this shows about the cabbage juice? You can check your results on page 47.

The pH Scale

The strength of an acid or base is measured on a scale called the **pH** scale, which goes from 0 to 14 in general usage. A few very strong acids and bases fall outside the scale. A liquid with a pH of 7 is neutral. A liquid with a pH lower than 7 is an acid. The lower the number, the more strongly acidic it is, so pH 6 is a very weak acid and pH 0 is a very strong acid. A liquid with a pH higher than 7 is a base. The higher the number, the more strongly **alkaline** it is, so pH 8 is a very weak alkali and pH 14 is a very strong alkali.

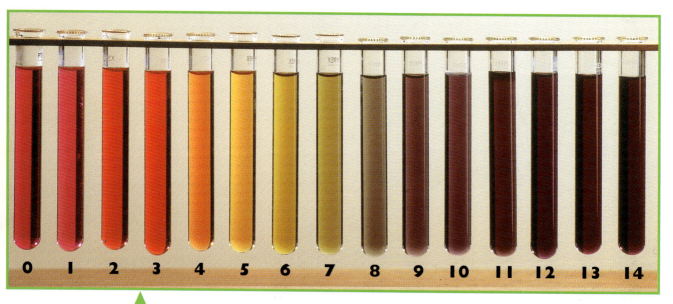

The test tubes contain acids (on the left) and alkalis (on the right) together with universal indicator solution. The strengths of the acids and alkalis are shown below as a pH number.

Universal indicator

An indicator called **universal indicator** shows the pH of a liquid. Like **litmus,** universal indicator comes in the form of paper strips, or as a **solution.** When it is put in a colorless liquid, it changes color to show how acidic or alkaline the liquid is. The pH is shown on a color-coded strip supplied with the indicator. Universal indicator is not good for testing colored liquids because the indicator may get some of its color from the liquid.

Demonstration: Using indicators

Here you will see how litmus paper and universal indicator paper can be used to test substances. The litmus paper and indicator paper change color to show whether a substance is an acid, a base, or neutral. The universal indicator paper can also tell you how strongly acidic or alkaline the substance is.

Demonstration Steps

1. Pour a small amount of a substance to test into a small jar.

> **EQUIPMENT**
> litmus paper (red and blue)
> universal indicator paper
> small jars
> substances to test, for example:
>   apple juice, white wine vinegar,
>   tap water, soap dissolved in a little
>   water, lemon juice, rainwater,
>   carbonated drinks, baking powder
>   dissolved in water, and/or
>   toothpaste dissolved in some
>   warm water

2. Dip a strip of red litmus paper into the liquid. If the dipped part turns blue, the substance is alkaline; if it stays red, it is either acidic or neutral. If it does stay red, dip a strip of blue litmus paper into it. If the dipped part turns red, it is acidic; if it stays blue, it is neutral. Repeat this process for each liquid and make a table of results.

3. Next, dip a strip of universal indicator paper into each liquid. Remove the papers and place each next to the color strip supplied with the book of paper. If there is no exact color match, estimate the pH of the solution. Add the results to your table.

Acid Reactions

When you put another substance into an acid, or pour an acid over another substance, a **chemical reaction** often happens between the acid and the substance. During the reaction, new substances are formed. There is always a consistent pattern of behavior to the reactions that happen between acids and other substances. For example, all acids react with the **metal** magnesium, and the products of the reaction are always hydrogen gas and a **compound** containing the magnesium. It doesn't matter what acid you use—the reaction will be the same. Sometimes there is no reaction between an acid and a substance. For example, some types of plastic never react with any acid. This is also a pattern of behavior.

Acids are used to dissolve scrap metal during the recycling process.

When you know the patterns of behavior that happen between acids and other substances, you can make a good guess about what is going to happen when you add an acid to a substance. You can also get some clues about what a mystery substance could be, by the reaction that occurs when you add acid to it. For example, if you added acid to a piece of metal and there was no hydrogen produced, then you could rule out the possibility of it being magnesium. So acids can be used as part of a series of laboratory tests on a substance.

Some useful reactions to know about are the reactions between acids and different metals; the reactions between acids and substances called **carbonates;** and the reactions between acids and bases or alkalis.

Reactions of acids and metals

When acids are added to some metals, the metals fizz and are eaten away. The fizzing is caused by tiny bubbles of hydrogen gas being formed—the hydrogen comes from the acid. The other part of the acid combines with the metal to make a compound called a **salt.** This is the general word equation for this reaction:

$$\text{acid + metal} \longrightarrow \text{salt + hydrogen}$$

Here is an example:

$$\text{hydrochloric acid + calcium} \longrightarrow \text{calcium chloride + hydrogen}$$
$$2HCl + Ca \longrightarrow CaCl_2 + H_2$$

The reaction between a metal and an acid is an example of a type of reaction called a **displacement reaction.** This is because the metal displaces, or takes the place of, the hydrogen in the acid. However, not all metals react with acids.

Strong acid has been used to etch patterns on these windows.

Experiment: Reactions of metals and acids

PROBLEM: What gas is produced when acids react with **metals?**

HYPOTHESIS: Acids contain hydrogen, so the gas produced may be hydrogen. If a flame is put in the gas, it should burn with a pop if it is hydrogen.

Experiment steps

1. Lay the plastic tube on its side in the box (or dish). Pour just enough vinegar into the box so that the plastic tube is completely filled with vinegar.

2. Put two or three nails into the plastic tube. Turn the plastic tube upside down so that the open end stays in the vinegar. If you do it carefully, the tube will stand on its end in the box, full of vinegar, and with the nails inside it.

3. After a short time, some bubbles of gas will start to come off the nail. Be patient. Wait until you have about one-half to one inch (one to two centimeters) of gas trapped in the top of your tube. This might take about 45 minutes.

4. Put the tube's lid into the vinegar. Lift the tube just enough to slide the lid into the open end—don't let any air get into the tube! Once the lid is on, take the tube out of the vinegar. Dry the outside of the tube, and wash your hands. You are now ready to test the gas to see if it is hydrogen.

5. Get an adult to help you with this step. You will only get one chance to get this right! Turn the tube upright so that the lid is at the top. Light a safety match, take the lid off the tube, and quickly hold the flame over the mouth of the tube. Listen carefully.

RESULTS: When you hold the flame next to the tube, what sort of sound do you hear? What do you think this tells you about the gas in the tube? You can check your results on page 47.

zinc	+	hydrochloric acid	$\longrightarrow$	zinc chloride	+	hydrogen
Zn	+	$2HCl$	$\longrightarrow$	$ZnCl_2$	+	H_2

The reactivity series

Different metals react with acids at different speeds. When acids are added to some metals, such as magnesium, there is lots of fizzing, showing that the reaction between the acid and metal is very fast. In fact some metals, such as potassium, react so violently that they cause an explosion. This is because the reaction produces so much heat that the hydrogen gas given off by the reaction explodes. When acids are added to other metals, such as iron, there is only slight fizzing. This shows that the reaction between the acid and the metal is slow. This difference in the speeds of the reactions is an example of a trend in **properties.** Some metals, such as gold, don't react with acids at all.

The **reactivity series** is a list of common metals in order of how fast they react with acids. The most reactive metals, such as potassium and sodium, are at the top, and the least reactive, such as gold and silver, are at the bottom.

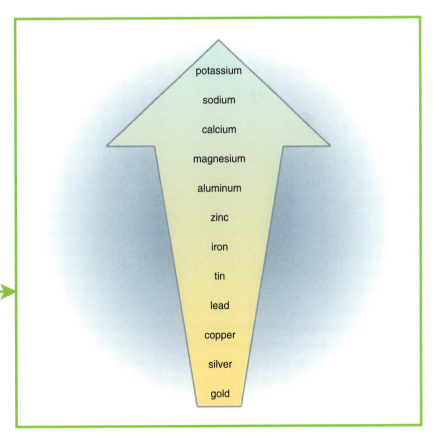

potassium
sodium
calcium
magnesium
aluminum
zinc
iron
tin
lead
copper
silver
gold

The reactivity series of common metals shows, for example, that aluminum is more reactive than zinc but less reactive than magnesium.

Reactivity

The **reactivity series** shows how reactive a **metal** is. The metals at the top of the series are very reactive, and those at the bottom are very unreactive. Each metal in the series is more reactive than the one below it.

If you look down the series below, you will see that there is a point at which metals stop reacting with acids. This is because a metal will react with an acid only if it is more reactive than hydrogen. If it is more reactive, a **displacement reaction** takes place, and the metal pushes the hydrogen out of the acid. If the metal is less reactive than hydrogen, then it cannot push the hydrogen out, and there is no reaction.

Hydrogen is often added to the reactivity series, even though it is not a metal. If an acid is added to a metal above hydrogen in the series, a reaction takes place and the metal displaces the hydrogen to make a **salt.** If an acid is added to a metal below hydrogen in the series, no reaction takes place.

Metal	Symbol	Reaction with acids
potassium	K	
sodium	Na	
calcium	Ca	
magnesium	Mg	All react
aluminum	Al	with acids
zinc	Zn	
iron	Fe	
lead	Pb	
hydrogen	H	
copper	Cu	
silver	Ag	No reaction
gold	Au	with acids

Experiment: Reactive metals

PROBLEM: Which common metals are most reactive?

HYPOTHESIS: To find which metals are most reactive, we can put pieces of the metals in a weak acid and watch what happens. The one that fizzes most quickly will be the most reactive.

Experiment steps

1. Put a nail or screw into each of the three small jars. Pour just enough vinegar into the jars to cover the nails or screws. Watch what happens over a few minutes. While you are waiting, ask an adult to heat a kettle of water (it does not need to boil).

2. Make sure a window is open because the next part can be really smelly! Ask the adult to pour some hot water into the bowl. Carefully put your jars into the water so that the hot water will heat up the vinegar in the jars. Again, watch what happens over a few minutes. Take care not to breathe deeply near the warm vinegar.

3. Make a note of your results. If bubbles are coming off the surface of the metal, there is a reaction happening. If you are not sure, gently swirl the vinegar to remove any bubbles. Then watch to see if they start forming on their own again. Write down whether the reaction is fast, steady, or slow, or if there is no reaction at all.

4. Write down the three metals in order of their speeds of reaction, starting your list with the most reactive and putting the least reactive last. This is your reactivity series.

RESULTS: Which of the metals fizzes most quickly? Which fizzes the least? What does this tell you about the reactivity of the different metals? You can check your results on page 47.

EQUIPMENT
nail or screw made of iron or steel
galvanized (zinc-coated) nail or screw
nail or screw made of copper or brass
white vinegar (colored vinegar will also work)
three small jars
one bowl (large enough to place all the jars into)

Acids and Carbonates

Just as there is a pattern of reactions between acids and **metals**, there is also a pattern of reactions between acids and certain **compounds** called **carbonates.** Carbonates are compounds created when **atoms** of one **element** combine with another group of atoms made up of one carbon atom and three oxygen atoms. One of the most common carbonates is calcium carbonate. It is found in rocks such as chalk, marble, and limestone. Its formula is $CaCO_3$, and it is the CO_3 part that makes it a carbonate.

When an acid is added to a carbonate, the carbonate fizzes. This is caused by the formation of bubbles of carbon dioxide gas in the reaction. Carbon dioxide is one of the products of the reaction. The other products are always water and a kind of compound called a **salt.**

Here is the general equation for the reaction:

acid + carbonate $\longrightarrow$ salt + water + carbon dioxide

For example, if hydrochloric acid is added to marble, which is made up of calcium carbonate, the marble fizzes as carbon dioxide gas is made.

hydrochloric acid	+	calcium carbonate	$\longrightarrow$	calcium chloride	+	water	+	carbon dioxide
$2HCl$	+	$CaCO_3$	$\longrightarrow$	$CaCl_2$	+	H_2O	+	CO_2

Bubbles of carbon dioxide rise from marble chips dropped into acid. The more powerful the acid, the faster the reaction happens.

Experiment: Reactions of acids and carbonates

PROBLEM: What gas is produced when acids react with carbonates?

HYPOTHESIS: All carbonates contain carbon and oxygen, so the gas released may be carbon dioxide. This can be tested by seeing if the gas causes a candle to stop burning.

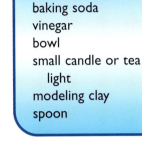

EQUIPMENT
baking soda
vinegar
bowl
small candle or tea
    light
modeling clay
spoon

Experiment steps

1. Ask an adult to help you with this experiment. Put a small candle in the bottom of the bowl and fasten it in place with some modeling clay. Make sure that the wick is well below the level of the bowl's rim. As an alternative, put a tea light in the bottom of the bowl.

2. Carefully pour vinegar into the bowl so that the candle is surrounded, but not covered. Ask the adult to light the candle with a match.

3. Add half a teaspoon of baking soda (bicarbonate of soda) to the vinegar and watch the flame carefully.

RESULTS: What happens to the flame? What do you think caused this? Think about what would be produced in such a reaction. You can check your results on page 47.

Neutralization

A neutral liquid is a liquid that is neither an acid nor a base. It has a **pH** of 7. An acid or a base can be turned into a neutral liquid by a certain type of **chemical reaction** called **neutralization.**

Neutralization happens when either an acid and a base, or an acid and an alkali, cancel each other out to make a neutral **solution.** The two most common neutralization reactions are between acids and bases called metal oxides, and between acids and alkalis called hydroxides. The products are always a **salt** and water. The general equation for these reactions is:

acid + base $\longrightarrow$ salt + water

Here is an example of the reaction between an acid and a hydroxide:

hydrochloric acid	+	sodium hydroxide	$\longrightarrow$	sodium chloride	+	water
HCl	+	$NaOH$	$\longrightarrow$	$NaCl$	+	H_2O

Here is an example of the reaction between an acid and a metal oxide:

hydrochloric acid	+	copper oxide	$\longrightarrow$	copper chloride	+	water
$2HCl$	+	CuO	$\longrightarrow$	$CuCl_2$	+	H_2O

Gradual neutralization

A base or an alkali will only neutralize an acid completely if enough of the base or alkali is added to the acid. If the base or alkali is added a bit at a time, the solution gradually becomes less acidic, and eventually all the acid is neutralized and the solution is neutral. If even more of the base is then added, the solution becomes **alkaline.**

Demonstration: A neutralization reaction

Here you can see how to neutralize an acid. By gradually adding an alkali and checking the pH of the solution, you will be able to tell when the solution becomes neutral.

Demonstration steps

1. Measure out about half a cup (100 mL) of water and pour it into a glass. Dissolve one level teaspoon of baking soda in this water. This is your alkali.

2. Put two teaspoons of vinegar into the measuring cup, and enough red cabbage **indicator** to get a nice red color. Add water to the mixture to get a total volume of half a cup (100 mL). Pour the colored mixture into the second glass. This is your acid.

3. Add one teaspoon of the colorless baking soda solution to your colored diluted vinegar, and stir. You may see some bubbles given off, but check the color of the mixture. Keep adding one teaspoon of baking soda solution, stirring each time, until the mixture changes to a blue color. When this happens, the vinegar has been neutralized and some extra alkali has been added. Note how many teaspoons of baking soda solution it took.

4. You now need to experiment to see exactly how much baking soda you need to get the mixture neutral. Wash out your colored mixture and make up some fresh vinegar and indicator mixture, following step 2. Repeat step 3, but stop before you add the last teaspoon. Add half a teaspoon instead and see if you get a blue color. If it turns blue, try the experiment again but add just a quarter of a teaspoon; if it does not turn blue, add another quarter of a teaspoon and see what happens. The goal is to get your experiment to the stage where just a tiny bit more baking soda solution would turn the mixture blue. You have neutralized the acid in the vinegar.

EQUIPMENT
two jars or glasses
small medicine spoon or
  kitchen measuring
  spoons
teaspoon
measuring cup
white wine vinegar
baking soda
red cabbage indicator
  (see page 15)

Making Salts

In chemistry, a **salt** is a substance made when an acid reacts with a base or an alkali. A salt is always a **compound** that contains a **metal** and a **nonmetal.** Table salt that we use in food is an example of a salt. Its chemical name is sodium chloride (NaCl), and it contains the metal sodium and the nonmetal chlorine. Other examples of salts are copper nitrate and iron sulfate.

A salt is made when the hydrogen in an acid is replaced by a metal. For example, when sodium replaces the hydrogen in hydrochloric acid, the salt sodium chloride is formed. When copper replaces the hydrogen in sulfuric acid, the salt copper sulfate is formed. Salts are named after the acid that forms them—for example, sulfates are formed from sulfuric acid, chlorides from hydrochloric acid, and nitrates from nitric acid.

Salts can be made by these four different reactions:

acid + metal	$\longrightarrow$	salt + hydrogen
acid + metal oxide (a base)	$\longrightarrow$	salt + water
acid + metal hydroxide (an alkali)	$\longrightarrow$	salt + water
acid + metal **carbonate**	$\longrightarrow$	salt + water + carbon dioxide

This Italian salt-producing plant is the largest in the country, providing 75 percent of the people's salt.

Experiment: Making a salt (sodium acetate)

PROBLEM: How can we produce a salt?

HYPOTHESIS: Salts are made when an acid reacts with an alkali or a base. We could try reacting a household acid and a household base together.

EQUIPMENT
two glass jars
strainer and paper towels
vinegar
baking soda
teaspoon
bowl
optional if you are in a hurry:
    saucepan and an adult

Experiment steps

1. Pour vinegar into a glass jar until it is about one-half to one inch (one to two centimeters) deep.

2. Put half a teaspoon of baking soda into the vinegar and stir it to mix. When the fizzing stops, add another half teaspoon of baking soda, and mix again. If it still fizzes, add more baking soda until there is no more fizzing. You should have some baking soda left in the bottom of the jar at this stage.

3. Filter your mixture into a bowl, using the strainer lined with two layers of paper towels. The liquid that comes through (called the filtrate) should be clear. If you see any solid in it, filter again.

4. Leave the bowl on a windowsill for a few days to let the water **evaporate.** This is the best method because you will get bigger crystals. If you do not have several days to carry out step 4, and do not mind getting very small crystals, ask an adult to help you as described in step 5.

5. Ask an adult to boil a small pan of water with your bowl of filtrate on top. The adult should adjust the heat to let the water in the pan simmer. When nearly all your filtrate has evaporated, let everything cool down. Look inside the bowl as it cools.

RESULTS: What has happened in the bowl? What do you think this substance is? You can check your results on page 47.

Acids in the Atmosphere

The air in Earth's **atmosphere** is a mixture of gases. About 99 percent of the air is made up of nitrogen and oxygen. In the remaining one percent is a very small amount of carbon dioxide. Carbon dioxide is an **acidic gas** that dissolves in water to make a weak acid called carbonic acid, with a **pH** of about six. The carbon dioxide in the atmosphere dissolves in the water droplets that make up clouds and rain. This means that rainwater is always slightly acidic. As it flows over some **metals** and also some types of rocks, it eats them away. It also makes the ground it falls on slightly acidic.

Chemical weathering

Chemical weathering is the wearing away of the rocks of Earth's crust by this slightly acidic rain. Rocks such as limestone and chalk are made up mainly of calcium **carbonate.** When acidic rainwater flows over these rocks, it reacts with the calcium carbonate to form a **salt** called calcium hydrogencarbonate.

$$\text{calcium carbonate} + \text{carbonic acid} \longrightarrow \text{calcium hydrogencarbonate}$$

$$CaCO_3 + H_2CO_3 \longrightarrow Ca(HCO_3)_2$$

When calcium hydrogencarbonate (known as calcium bicarbonate) drips slowly, it deposits calcium carbonate, forming stalactites and stalagmites.

The calcium hydrogencarbonate (calcium bicarbonate) dissolves in water and is carried away, often creating huge underground caverns in limestone rocks. However, where water containing dissolved calcium bicarbonate drips slowly from a surface, the reaction above can reverse, meaning that calcium carbonate is deposited. Over many years, this can build up to create amazing rock formations called **stalagmites** and **stalactites.** The scale inside a kettle is formed in the same way.

Acid rain

Scientists use the term acid rain to describe rainwater that is more acidic than natural rainwater. It is caused by acidic gases released into the atmosphere when **fossil fuels** are burned in factories, power plants, and vehicle engines. The gases produced include sulfur dioxide and oxides of nitrogen. When these gases dissolve in rainwater, they form acids that are stronger than carbonic acid.

Acid rain from burning fossil fuels is more harmful than natural rain because it eats away rocks quickly and damages the stone on buildings and statues. It also reacts with metals such as steel, weakening objects made from them. Acid rain can kill plants and animals where it falls regularly in the same place and where it flows into rivers and lakes. The amount of acidic gases released into the atmosphere can be reduced by devices such as catalytic converters in cars, or by removing impurities such as sulfur from fuels before they are used.

The water in the soil around these plants has become strongly acidic because of acid rain. The trees cannot grow in such conditions.

Using Acids and Bases

Many acids, alkalis, and bases are very useful. So are the reactions they take part in and the products of these reactions. We use these substances at home for cooking and cleaning, and in industry for processing materials and for making other chemicals.

Acid and alkali cleaners

Some cleaning liquids contain acids. **Descalers** are a good example—they are chemicals specifically designed to remove scale from inside kettles and water heaters. Scale, sometimes called limescale, is a layer of calcium **carbonate** that has been deposited from tap water. It does not **dissolve** in water, so you cannot clean it away with just water. It comes from the rocks through which the water has flowed. There is acid in the descaler that reacts with the scale, turning it into a **salt** called calcium bicarbonate. This salt does dissolve in water and then gets washed away. A descaler is a weak acid that does not react with the kettle or water heater itself. Other household cleaners use stronger acids. They can be used to remove thick scale from materials that do not react with acids, such as glass and ceramics.

Strong alkalis such as sodium hydroxide are used in oven cleaners because they are very **corrosive.** They react with grease in the oven and turn it into simpler chemicals that can be washed away with water. Ammonia **solution** (made by dissolving ammonia gas in water), is a weak alkali, and it is a common ingredient in cleaning agents such as spray-on kitchen surface cleaners. Many soaps and detergents contain alkalis, too.

This special cleaner reacts with the dull silver oxide coating on silver, making it clean and shiny again.

The holes in bread are full of carbon dioxide gas, created by reactions of acids and bases.

Acids and bases in cooking

Vinegar contains a weak acid called acetic acid. The **microorganisms** that feed on food and make it spoil cannot live in acid, so foods such as onions can be put in vinegar to preserve them. The vinegar soaks into the food, killing any microorganisms. This process of preserving food was very popular before refrigerators were invented.

Baking soda is an ingredient added to bread and cakes to make them rise. It contains the salt sodium bicarbonate, also called sodium hydrogencarbonate or bicarbonate of soda. When it is heated, it gives off carbon dioxide that expands, making bubbles in the dough or cake mixture. Some baking powders also contain acidic solids. When the baking soda is mixed into a cake, it becomes wet. At the same time, an acid is formed that reacts with the bicarbonate, and carbon dioxide is made.

Acids and Bases in Industry

Huge amounts of acids, bases, and alkalis are made and used every year by industries. Acids, bases, and alkalis, and chemicals produced from them, are made at chemical plants. The plants are a maze of tanks and pipes, but they often do the same job as more simple equipment that you see in a laboratory—just on a much larger scale. **Chemical reactions** happen in the tanks, often at high temperatures and pressures, making the reactions happen faster and more efficiently.

Industrial acids

The most important industrial acid is sulfuric acid. It has many uses, such as cleaning and purifying **metals** or making other industrial acids, such as phosphoric acids and nitric acid. Steel is cleaned thoroughly with sulfuric acid before it is galvanized (coated with zinc) to protect it from rusting.

The other main industrial acids are nitric acid and hydrochloric acid. Nitric acid is used to manufacture nitrate **fertilizers** and explosives such as nitroglycerin. Hydrochloric acid is used mainly for purifying metals.

*This chemical plant in Cumbria, England, produces chemicals, including sulfuric acid for use in **detergents**, soap, toothpaste, and foams.*

Industrial bases and alkalis

The most important industrial bases and alkalis are sodium hydroxide and sodium **carbonate,** both made from table **salt** (sodium chloride). Sodium hydroxide has many uses, such as making other chemicals, synthetic fibers, and soaps. The main use of sodium carbonate is in glass-making.

Making fertilizers

The greatest use of nitric acids and phosphoric acids is in making fertilizers that farmers put on their fields to make crops grow better. The acids are made to react with alkalis, such as ammonia, to create salts.

Fertilizer often comes as pellets, like these being loaded into a container for transport. Farmers sprinkle the pellets onto their fields, where they dissolve in rainwater and wash into the soil.

Making sulfuric acid

Sulfuric acid is the most widely used chemical in industry. Hundreds of millions of tons of it are manufactured every year. Sulfuric acid is made using a process called the contact process. First, sulfur and oxygen are reacted together to make sulfur dioxide. This then reacts with more oxygen using a catalyst to make sulfur trioxide. The sulfur trioxide is dissolved in sulfuric acid to make an extremely **concentrated** form of sulfuric acid called oleum. The oleum is stored, ready to be **diluted** to make acid for industry and laboratories.

Useful Neutralization

As we have seen, **neutralization** is a chemical reaction in which an acid is neutralized by a base or an alkali, or in which an alkali is neutralized by an acid. Many acids, bases, and alkalis are used for neutralization reactions that can be useful in everyday life.

Controlling acidity

One of the important **properties** of a soil is how acidic or **alkaline** it is. Different species of plants grow well in different places, including those with acidic soils, neutral soils, or alkaline soils. Gardeners and farmers often have to treat their soil to change its **pH** so that their crops will grow well.

Some soils have a pH as low as four or even three! To make soil less acidic, gardeners and farmers mix in a base called calcium oxide, also called lime or slaked lime. Lime is also added to land and lakes that have been made so acidic by acid rain that animals and plants are being killed.

This farmer is spreading lime (calcium oxide) onto his fields. Rain will wash the lime into the soil and reduce its acidity.

Treating stings

Insect and nettle stings hurt because the sting injects either acid or alkali into your skin. However, they can be made less painful by neutralizing the acid or alkali. Bee, ant, and nettle stings are acidic, so you can treat them with an alkali. Wasp stings, on the other hand, contain alkali, so you can treat them with a weak acid such as vinegar. Never use strong laboratory acids on a sting!

Experiment: Testing antacid tablets

PROBLEM: Which antacid tablets neutralize hydrochloric acid best?

HYPOTHESIS: Antacid tablets contain bases that neutralize excess hydrochloric acid in your stomach. Testing how much an antacid tablet neutralizes a measured amount of acid will show how effective it is.

Experiment steps

1. Put one of the antacid tablets onto the paper. Fold the paper over the tablet and use the back of the spoon to crush the tablet.

2. Pour some white wine vinegar into a small jar until the vinegar is about an inch (three centimeters) deep. Add some cabbage **indicator** and make a note of the color of the mixture.

3. Open the paper and use the tip of the spoon to add a small amount of crushed tablet to the jar. Watch the reaction and make a note of the color of the mixture.

4. Repeat steps 2 and 3 for each different brand of antacid tablet you have, using the same amount of vinegar each time.

5. You can extend your investigation by trying different tablets to see which ones neutralize the acids with the smallest amount of tablet (do this by adding small amounts of tablet until there is no further reaction). You can also try **universal indicator solution** or paper, if you can get it.

RESULTS: Which tablet produces the greatest change in color? What do you think this means about its ability to neutralize acid? You can check your results on page 47.

> **EQUIPMENT**
> small jar
> white wine vinegar
> different kinds of antacid tablets
> cabbage indicator (see page 15)
> piece of paper
> spoon

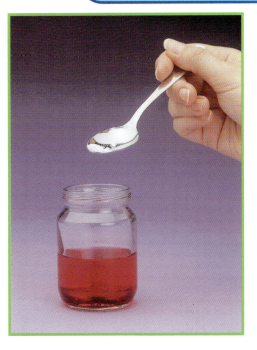

Useful Salts

A **salt** is a **compound** containing a **metal** and a **nonmetal,** such as sodium chloride (table salt) and copper sulfate. All salts are made up of crystals, and they have a huge range of uses both at home and in industry. Here are a few examples.

Table salt

The salt that we put on food is table salt, with the chemical name sodium chloride. Besides improving the flavor of some foods, it is an important part of our diet. It is also used for preserving food because it can kill **microorganisms** when it is very concentrated. In industry, sodium chloride is used to make sodium hydroxide, sodium **carbonate,** chlorine, and hydrochloric acid. Rock salt is mostly sodium chloride, and it is spread on roads to keep them free of ice in cold weather.

Finding salt

Sodium chloride, or table salt, is obtained in two very different ways—from sea water and by mining. Sea water is 2.7 percent sodium chloride, dissolved in the water. To get the sodium chloride from the water, the water is **evaporated,** leaving the salt behind. Most salt comes from mines. It is found in deposits called rock salt, and is dug out and crushed into powder by machines. Rock salt is also removed from the ground by pumping water into the rock. The water dissolves the salt and is then pumped to the surface again, where it is evaporated, leaving the salt.

These pools are called salt pans. Sea water is poured onto them, and salt is gradually left behind as the water evaporates.

Salts in medicine

If you have ever broken an arm or a leg, a salt called calcium sulfate was probably used to make the cast around it while it mended. Calcium sulfate is also known as plaster of Paris. Zinc carbonate, also known as calamine, is used to help to soothe sore or itchy skin. Iron tablets contain iron sulfate, and the iron in them makes your blood better at carrying oxygen around your body. Magnesium sulfate is an ingredient in constipation remedies.

Salts on the farm

All **fertilizers** are made up of salts, most often nitrates and phosphates made from nitric and phosphoric acids. The most common are ammonium nitrate, ammonium phosphate, sodium nitrate, and potassium nitrate. The salts contain nitrogen, phosphorus, and potassium that the crops need to grow. Fertilizers usually come as pellets that are sprinkled on fields. They dissolve in rainwater and are washed into the soil, where they are taken in by the plants' roots.

Phosphates and nitrates are used to manufacture explosives, such as the ones used in quarries.

The Periodic Table

The periodic table is a chart of all the known **elements.** The elements are arranged in order of their atomic numbers, but in rows, so that elements with similar **properties** are underneath each other. The periodic table gets its name from the fact that the elements' properties repeat themselves every few elements, or periodically. The position of an element in the periodic table gives an idea of what its properties are likely to be.

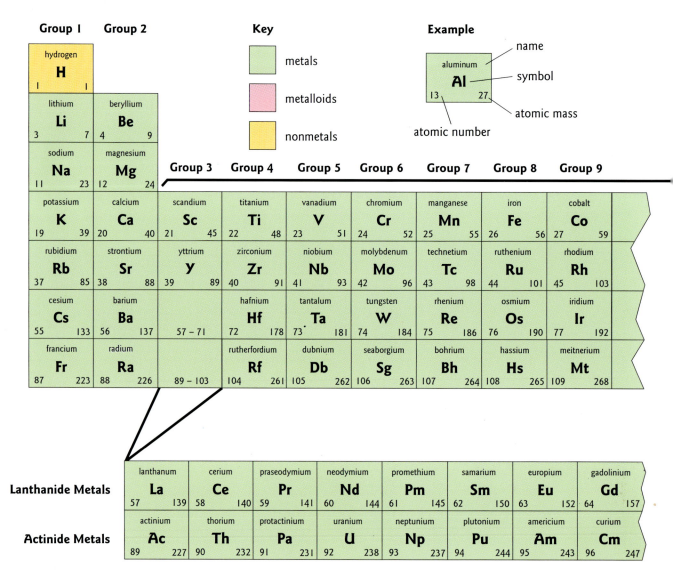

Key
- metals
- metalloids
- nonmetals

Example

aluminum — name
Al — symbol
13 — atomic number
27 — atomic mass

Group 1	Group 2	Group 3	Group 4	Group 5	Group 6	Group 7	Group 8	Group 9
hydrogen **H** 1, 1								
lithium **Li** 3, 7	beryllium **Be** 4, 9							
sodium **Na** 11, 23	magnesium **Mg** 12, 24							
potassium **K** 19, 39	calcium **Ca** 20, 40	scandium **Sc** 21, 45	titanium **Ti** 22, 48	vanadium **V** 23, 51	chromium **Cr** 24, 52	manganese **Mn** 25, 55	iron **Fe** 26, 56	cobalt **Co** 27, 59
rubidium **Rb** 37, 85	strontium **Sr** 38, 88	yttrium **Y** 39, 89	zirconium **Zr** 40, 91	niobium **Nb** 41, 93	molybdenum **Mo** 42, 96	technetium **Tc** 43, 98	ruthenium **Ru** 44, 101	rhodium **Rh** 45, 103
cesium **Cs** 55, 133	barium **Ba** 56, 137	57 – 71	hafnium **Hf** 72, 178	tantalum **Ta** 73, 181	tungsten **W** 74, 184	rhenium **Re** 75, 186	osmium **Os** 76, 190	iridium **Ir** 77, 192
francium **Fr** 87, 223	radium **Ra** 88, 226	89 – 103	rutherfordium **Rf** 104, 261	dubnium **Db** 105, 262	seaborgium **Sg** 106, 263	bohrium **Bh** 107, 264	hassium **Hs** 108, 265	meitnerium **Mt** 109, 268

Lanthanide Metals

lanthanum **La** 57, 139	cerium **Ce** 58, 140	praseodymium **Pr** 59, 141	neodymium **Nd** 60, 144	promethium **Pm** 61, 145	samarium **Sm** 62, 150	europium **Eu** 63, 152	gadolinium **Gd** 64, 157

Actinide Metals

actinium **Ac** 89, 227	thorium **Th** 90, 232	protactinium **Pa** 91, 231	uranium **U** 92, 238	neptunium **Np** 93, 237	plutonium **Pu** 94, 244	americium **Am** 95, 243	curium **Cm** 96, 247

Groups and periods

The vertical columns of elements are called groups. The horizontal rows of elements are called periods. Some groups have special names:

Group 1: Alkali **metals**
Group 2: **Alkaline** earth metals
Groups 3–12: Transition metals
Group 17: Halogens
Group 18: Noble gases

The table is divided into two main sections, the metals and **nonmetals.** Between the two are elements that have some properties of metals and some of nonmetals. They are called semimetals or **metalloids.**

Group 13	Group 14	Group 15	Group 16	Group 17	Group 18
					helium **He** 2 · 4
boron **B** 5 · 11	carbon **C** 6 · 12	nitrogen **N** 7 · 14	oxygen **O** 8 · 16	fluorine **F** 9 · 19	neon **Ne** 10 · 20
aluminum **Al** 13 · 27	silicon **Si** 14 · 28	phosphorus **P** 15 · 31	sulfur **S** 16 · 32	chlorine **Cl** 17 · 35	argon **Ar** 18 · 40

Group 10	Group 11	Group 12						
nickel **Ni** 28 · 59	copper **Cu** 29 · 64	zinc **Zn** 30 · 65	gallium **Ga** 31 · 70	germanium **Ge** 32 · 73	arsenic **As** 33 · 75	selenium **Se** 34 · 79	bromine **Br** 35 · 80	krypton **Kr** 36 · 84
palladium **Pd** 46 · 106	silver **Ag** 47 · 108	cadmium **Cd** 48 · 112	indium **In** 49 · 115	tin **Sn** 50 · 119	antimony **Sb** 51 · 122	tellurium **Te** 52 · 128	iodine **I** 53 · 127	xenon **Xe** 54 · 131
platinum **Pt** 78 · 195	gold **Au** 79 · 197	mercury **Hg** 80 · 201	thallium **Tl** 81 · 204	lead **Pb** 82 · 207	bismuth **Bi** 83 · 209	polonium **Po** 84 · 209	astatine **At** 85 · 210	radon **Rn** 86 · 222
unununnilium **Uun** 110 · 281	unununium **Uuu** 111 · 272	ununbium **Uub** 112 · 285		ununquadium **Uuq** 114 · 289				

terbium **Tb** 65 · 159	dysprosium **Dy** 66 · 163	holmium **Ho** 67 · 165	erbium **Er** 68 · 167	thulium **Tm** 69 · 169	ytterbium **Yb** 70 · 173	lutetium **Lu** 71 · 175
berkelium **Bk** 97 · 247	californium **Cf** 98 · 251	einsteinium **Es** 99 · 252	fermium **Fm** 100 · 257	mendelevium **Md** 101 · 258	nobelium **No** 102 · 259	lawrencium **Lr** 103 · 262

Common Elements

Here is a table of common **elements** from the periodic table that you may find at home or in a laboratory. The table indicates whether the element is a **metal, nonmetal,** or **metalloid,** and whether it is a solid, liquid, or gas at room temperature.

Element	Symbol	Metal or not	State at room temperature
hydrogen	H	nonmetal	gas
helium	He	nonmetal	gas
lithium	Li	metal	solid
carbon	C	nonmetal	solid
nitrogen	N	nonmetal	gas
oxygen	O	nonmetal	gas
fluorine	F	nonmetal	gas
neon	Ne	nonmetal	gas
sodium	Na	metal	solid
magnesium	Mg	metal	solid
aluminum	Al	metal	solid
silicon	Si	metalloid	solid
phosphorus	P	nonmetal	solid
sulfur	S	nonmetal	solid
chlorine	Cl	nonmetal	gas
argon	Ar	nonmetal	gas
potassium	K	metal	solid
calcium	Ca	metal	solid
iron	Fe	metal	solid
copper	Cu	metal	solid
zinc	Zn	metal	solid
bromine	Br	nonmetal	liquid
silver	Ag	metal	solid
tin	Sn	metal	solid
iodine	I	nonmetal	solid
gold	Au	metal	solid
mercury	Hg	metal	liquid
lead	Pb	metal	solid

Common Chemicals

Here is a table of some common chemicals that you may come across at home or in the laboratory. The middle column shows their **chemical formulas.**

Chemical	Symbol	Components
Gases		
hydrogen	H_2	hydrogen
oxygen	O_2	oxygen
chlorine	Cl_2	chlorine
nitrogen	N_2	nitrogen
carbon dioxide	CO_2	carbon, oxygen
nitrogen dioxide	NO_2	nitrogen, oxygen
Liquids and solutions		
water	H_2O	hydrogen, oxygen
hydrochloric acid	HCl	hydrogen, chlorine
sulfuric acid	H_2SO_4	hydrogen, sulfur, oxygen
nitric acid	HNO_3	hydrogen, nitrogen, oxygen
sodium hydroxide	$NaOH$	sodium, oxygen, hydrogen
Solids		
sodium chloride	$NaCl$	sodium, chlorine
magnesium oxide	MgO	magnesium, oxygen
calcium carbonate	$CaCO_3$	calcium, carbon, oxygen
copper sulfate	$CuSO_4$	copper, sulfur, oxygen

Glossary

acidic gas gas that dissolves in water to make an acid. Hydrogen chloride is an acidic gas. It dissolves in water to make hydrochloric acid.

alkaline describes a liquid that has a pH above 7. All alkalis are alkaline. Alkaline also describes solids or gases that dissolve in water to make alkalis.

atmosphere blanket of air that surrounds Earth

atom extremely tiny particle of matter. An atom is the smallest particle of an element that can exist and still have all the properties of that element. All substances are made up of atoms.

carbonate compound made up of atoms of one element combined with another group of atoms made up of one carbon atom and three oxygen atoms

caustic causing corrosion or burning

chemical formula collection of symbols and numbers that represents an element or compound. It shows what elements are in a compound and the ratio of the numbers of atoms of each element.

chemical reaction sequence that happens when two chemicals (called the reactants) react together to form new chemicals (called the products)

compound substance made up of two or more different elements joined together by chemical bonds

concentrated containing a high amount of solute compared to the amount of solvent in a solution

corrosive tending to eat away other substances. Strong acids and strong alkalis are corrosive.

descaler chemical that removes scale that has formed inside water containers such as kettles

detergent chemical that breaks down oil and grease. Detergents are used for cleaning, and are contained in liquids and powders for washing dishes and clothing.

digestion process of breaking down food into simple substances that the body can use

dilute containing a small amount of solute compared to the amount of solvent in a solution

displacement reaction chemical reaction in which one of the elements in a compound is pushed out, or displaced, from the compound by another element. Some metals displace the hydrogen in an acid when they are put in the acid.

dissolve when the particles of a solid mix with those of a liquid so they disappear into the liquid

element substance that contains just one type of atom. Elements are the simplest substances that exist.

evaporate to change from liquid to gas at a temperature below the liquid's boiling point

fertilizer chemical that contains elements such as nitrogen and potassium, which plants need in order to grow

fossil fuel natural fuel such as coal or gas, formed over thousands of years from the remains of living things

indicator substance that changes color to show whether the liquid it is put in is acidic or alkaline. Some indicators also show how strongly acidic or alkaline a liquid is.

insoluble base base that does not dissolve in water. Insoluble bases can still neutralize acids.

litmus chemical extracted from lichens that acts as an indicator. Red litmus paper turns blue in an alkali or base. Blue litmus paper turns red in an acid.

metal any element in the periodic table that is shiny, and that conducts electricity and heat well. Most metals are also hard.

microorganism living thing that is too small to see without a microscope

neutralize to produce a chemical reaction that makes an acid, alkali, or base into a neutral liquid. Acids are neutralized by alkalis and bases. Alkalis and bases are neutralized by acids.

nonmetal any element in the periodic table that is not a metal or metalloid. Most nonmetals are gases.

organism single living thing

pH scale of the acidity or alkalinity of a liquid. A liquid with a pH less than 7 is an acid. A liquid with a pH greater than 7 is a base. A liquid with a pH of 7 is neutral.

property characteristic of a substance, such as its color, feel, melting point, or density

raw material simple material that is made into more complex materials or objects

reactivity series list of common metals arranged in order of how quickly they react with other substances, such as acids, water, and air. The most reactive metals are at the top.

salt substance made when an acid reacts with an alkali or a base. A salt is always a compound that contains a metal and one or more nonmetals.

solution substance made when a solid, gas, or liquid (the solute) dissolves in another solid, gas, or liquid (the solvent)

stalactite column of calcium carbonate that grows down from the roof of a cave

stalagmite column of calcium carbonate that grows up from the floor of a cave

universal indicator indicator that shows the strength of an acid or base. Universal indicator comes in paper and liquid form.

Experiment Results

page 15: The cabbage juice turns a different color in the tap water and in the weak acid. This shows that it works as an indicator.

pages 20–21: When you hold the flame over the mouth of the tube you should hear a popping sound. This shows that the gas produced was hydrogen, which burned when the flame was close to it. Hydrogen often burns so quickly that it explodes—this is the popping sound you hear. When metals react with acids, they produce hydrogen.

page 23: The zinc nail will fizz most quickly, so it is the most reactive. Iron will fizz a little bit, and the copper nail will not fizz at all. It is the least reactive.

page 25: The flame should go out. This is caused by the gas produced during the reaction. The carbonate contains carbon and oxygen, and carbon dioxide does not support burning, so the gas is probably carbon dioxide.

page 29: Crystals of a solid will form in the bowl. This solid must be the salt sodium acetate, formed in the reaction between the acetic acid in the vinegar and the sodium bicarbonate in the baking soda.

page 37: The tablet that produces the greatest change in color is the best at neutralizing the acid.

Further Reading

Fullick, Ann. *Chemicals in Action*. Chicago: Heinemann Library, 1999.

Gardner, Robert. *Science Project Ideas about Kitchen Chemistry*. Berkeley Heights, N.J.: Enslow Publishers, Inc., 2002.

Moje, Steven W. *Cool Chemistry: Great Experiments with Simple Stuff*. Madison, Wisc.: Turtleback Books, 2001.

Oxlade, Chris. *Illustrated Dictionary of Chemistry*. Tulsa, Okla.: EDC Publishing, 2000.

Stwertka, Albert, and Eve Stwertka. *A Guide to the Elements*. New York: Oxford University Press, 1999.

Index